My First Book of
Ballet

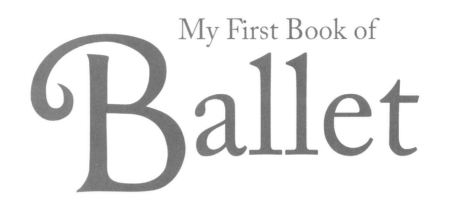

Cupcake is an imprint of Alligator Books Ltd
Gadd House, Arcadia Avenue
London N3 2JU

With thanks to the Dorothy Coleborn School of Dancing, Bath, UK

Project Director: Christine Swift
Dancers: Ruby Jones • Freya Catchpool • Meg Anderson
Harriet Edmonds • Mischa Eckersley • Opal Edmonds
Candice Fotheringham (Teacher)
Project Consultant: Annette Hind
Wardrobe: Annabel Hall • Hair: Carole Sherringham-Smith
Photographer: Sarah Merson Photography Ltd • Author: Lia Foa
Editor: Elise See Tai

Contents

Introduction

Ballet is a form of dance that is graceful, beautiful and magical to watch.

Becoming a good ballerina takes time, practice and dedication. Most importantly, it takes a love of the dance!

This book will introduce you to the basics of ballet. You will be able to try ballet positions and exercises that can develop your strength, flexibility, grace and balance.

Your ballet shoes should fit like a glove.

Stretching is important to warm up your muscles.

On stage, ballerinas wear an array of stunning outfits, but in the ballet studio it's a different matter. While practicing, even professional ballerinas wear simple clothes that allow their teacher to see their bodies and check that they are moving correctly.

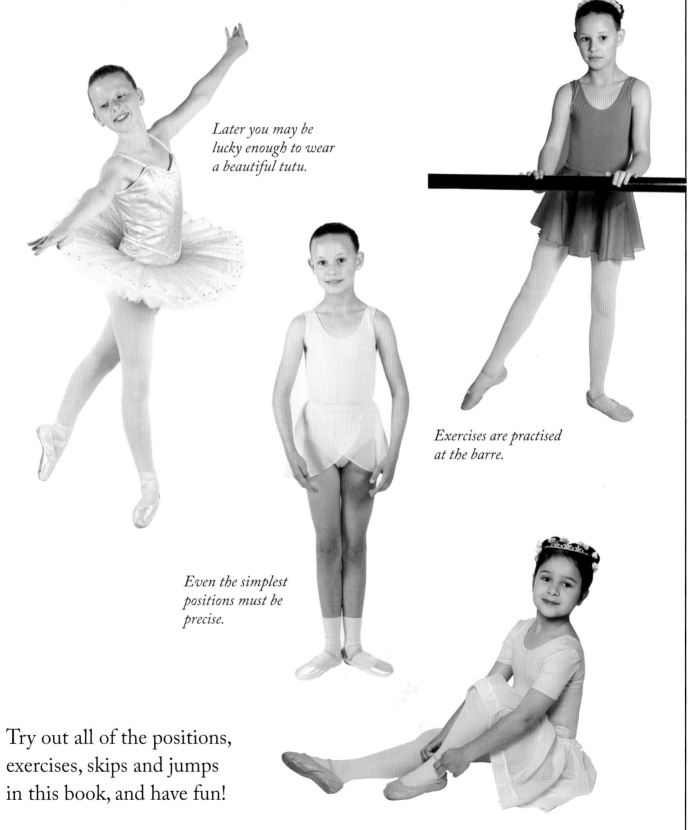

Later you may be lucky enough to wear a beautiful tutu.

Exercises are practised at the barre.

Even the simplest positions must be precise.

Try out all of the positions, exercises, skips and jumps in this book, and have fun!

Ballet Bag

Brush, hair pins and bands:
Keep your hair neatly pulled back
for class.

Ballet shoes: Initially, ballet dancers
wear flat shoes made from leather
or canvas, with elastic to hold them
in place. Your ballet shoes should fit
your feet perfectly, like a glove.

Leotard: A simple leotard is the best
item of clothing to wear in class as it
is comfortable and allows your body
to move easily.

Socks/Tights: It is best to wear socks
or tights when you begin to learn
ballet so that the teacher can see the
muscles in your legs to check that
they are working correctly.

Skirt: A short skirt is sometimes
tied around the waist.

Posture

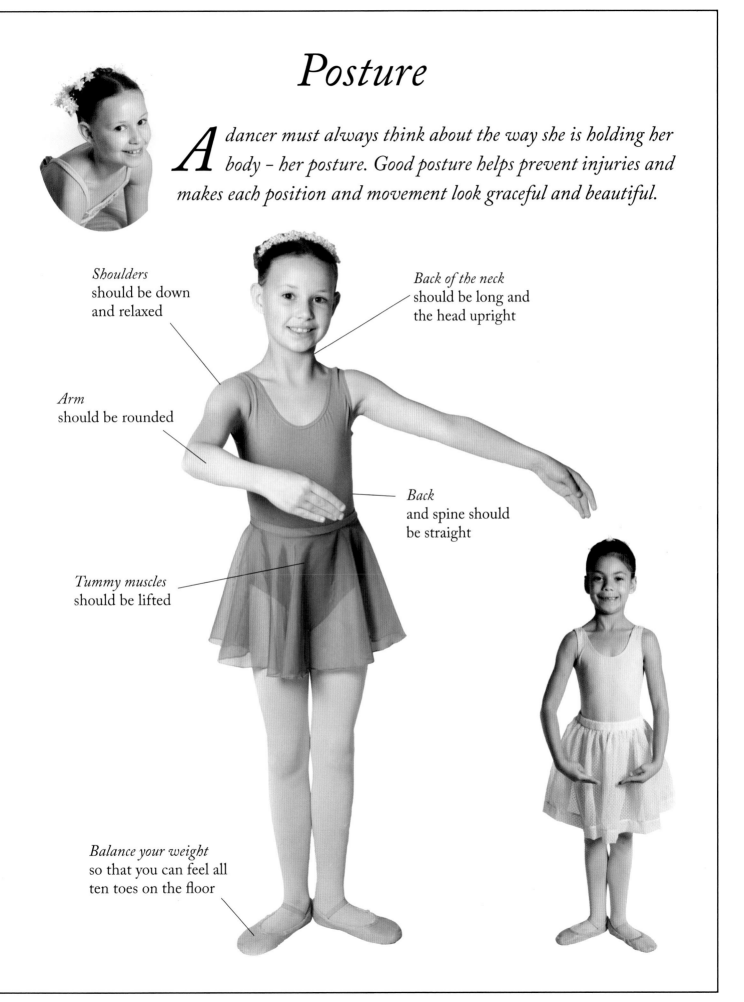

A dancer must always think about the way she is holding her body – her posture. Good posture helps prevent injuries and makes each position and movement look graceful and beautiful.

Shoulders
should be down
and relaxed

Back of the neck
should be long and
the head upright

Arm
should be rounded

Back
and spine should
be straight

Tummy muscles
should be lifted

Balance your weight
so that you can feel all
ten toes on the floor

Feet

*E*very movement in ballet, from a simple sauté (jump), to an advanced pirouette (turn), makes use of the basic ballet positions. Try each of the five positions of the feet demonstrated here. The more you practice, the better you'll get.

1st Position

- Place your heels together and turn your toes out to the sides as much as possible.

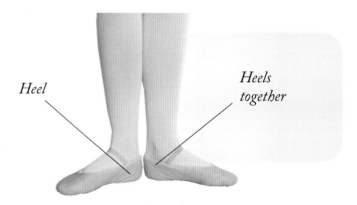

Heel

Heels together

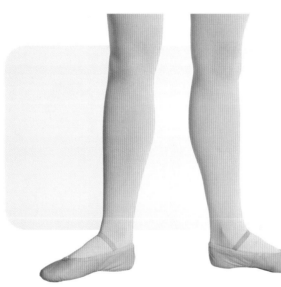

2nd Position

- From 1st position, step out with one foot so that your feet are about one foot length apart.

- Keep your legs turned out.

3rd Position

- From 1st position, slide one foot half way along the other foot, so that the heel of the front foot is touching the instep of the back foot.

- Keep your weight balanced between your feet.

Instep

4TH POSITION

- From 3rd position, slide your front foot forward.

- Your toes should be facing away from each other.

- Try not to twist your body.

- Keep both feet turned out as much as you can.

- Leave a gap of one foot length between your feet.

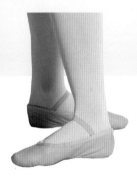

5TH POSITION

- This is similar to 3rd position.

- Slide the heel along so that it touches the base of your big toe.

- Turn out your feet as much as you can.

Your ballet teacher will be able to help you put your feet in the right position.

Beginning

*B*allerinas spend a lot of time practicing exercises that help them to become more flexible and stronger – all of which helps improve their dancing. Exercises are also good to help warm the muscles. These simple exercises will help you to warm up.

HELLO TOES AND GOODBYE TOES

This is a great exercise to warm up and stretch your feet!

- Sit with your legs straight out in front of you.
- Rest your hands on your legs or just behind you and sit up as straight as you can.
- Now gently stretch your feet away from you and point your toes (hello toes).

Keep your knees straight

- Then, bring your toes back up as far as you can.
- These are your goodbye toes.

FROG
This is a really good exercise to help you turn out your legs. Try to get your knees as near to the floor as you can, but NEVER push.

Just keep practicing!

STRETCH
This exercise stretches your neck, spine, arms and legs.

- Start by sitting up straight, then slowly relax forward towards your legs.
- Keep your bottom and your legs flat on the floor.
- Be careful to stretch only as far as you feel comfortable.
- To begin with, hold your knees or calves with your hands.

Later, you may be flexible enough to touch your toes!

Arms

*M*ovements of the arms add grace, expression and beauty to a dance. Just like the basic positions of the feet, these arm positions will be used in every new sequence you learn.

Bras Bas

This is the starting position for your arms. Hold them a little in front of your body and relax them into a gentle curve. Try to make an oval shape with your arms, while keeping your shoulders relaxed.

1st Position

- Raise your arms from bras bas until they are level with your tummy.
- This is 1st position. You usually move through 1st position to get to the other arm positions.

Always remember to relax your shoulders, keep your fingers relaxed and together, and to support your elbows.

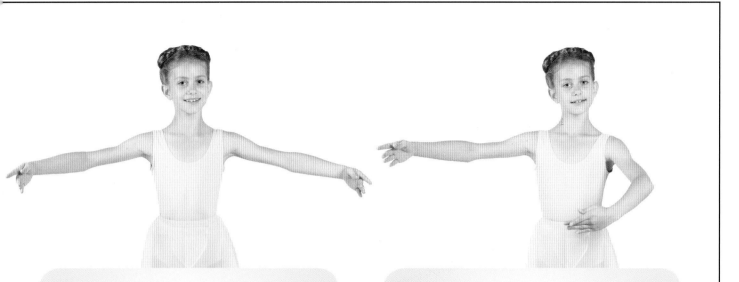

2ND POSITION

- From 1st position, open your arms wide into 2nd position.

- In this position your arms should be slightly below your shoulder height.

3RD POSITION

- In this position one arm is held in 1st and the other floats out into 2nd.

4TH POSITION

- From 1st position, take one arm up above your head, making a graceful 4th position.

- Your raised arm is held slightly in front of your head.

5TH POSITION

- Now raise both arms up above your head and hold them just in front of your body in an oval shape.

- You will have to try hard not to lift your shoulders in this position.

Port de Bras

*B*allet dancers gracefully move their arms through different positions as they dance – this is called port de bras, in French, which means 'carriage of the arms'.

Different ballet schools have special *port de bras* sequences, but you can create your own by elegantly moving your arms through the positions you've learned, in time to music.

1st position

2nd position

3rd position

4th position

5th position

Demi-pliés

*D*emi-pliés are among the first ballet movements you will learn. They build up strength, flexibility and balance, and are the foundation for every turn, jump and safety landing as you dance.

DEMI-PLIÉ IN 1ST POSITION

- Stand with your feet in 1st position, with your body straight and tall.

- Bend your knees over your toes to create a diamond shape between your legs.

- Bend your legs as far as you can, making sure your heels stay flat on the floor.

- Stretch up again, closing your legs and bringing your knees tightly together.

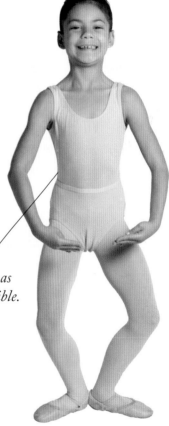

Keep your back as straight as possible.

DEMI-PLIÉ IN 2ND POSITION

- Start with your feet in 2nd position.

- Bend your knees sideways and go halfway down, while keeping your heels on the floor.

- Straighten your legs back up again.

Demi-pliés can be carried out in all five positions.

Battement Tendu at the Barre

The battement tendu is one of the most important exercises for developing your ballet technique. It teaches you to move your legs and feet correctly, and increases strength, the turn out of your legs, and also control in your legs.

À LA SECONDE
À la seconde means to the side.

- Stand with your feet in 1st position, holding the barre with one hand.

- Slide one foot out to the side, raising your heel and pointing your toes to the floor.

- Try to make a straight line through your stretched knee, instep and toes.

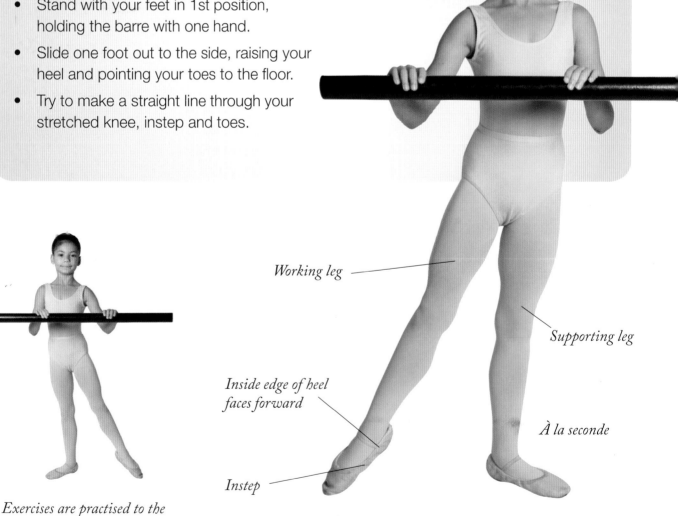

Working leg

Supporting leg

Inside edge of heel faces forward

À la seconde

Instep

Exercises are practised to the left and to the right.

DEVANT

Devant means 'in front'.

- Start in 1st position, with the barre to the side of you.
- Stretch your leg forward until your heel lifts off of the floor.
- Keep stretching until you are just touching the floor.
- Return to 1st position again.

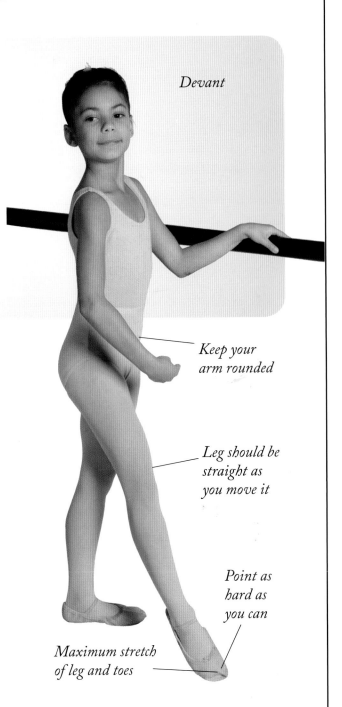

Devant

Keep your arm rounded

Leg should be straight as you move it

Point as hard as you can

Maximum stretch of leg and toes

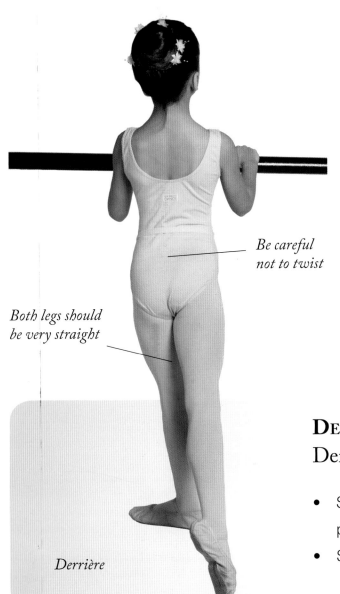

Be careful not to twist

Both legs should be very straight

Derrière

DERRIÈRE

Derrière means 'behind'.

- Stand facing the barre with your feet in 1st position.
- Slide one leg back, leading with the toes.

Jumps

*W*hen a ballerina jumps into the air, she appears to be as light and delicate as a feather, and lands with barely a sound. See how light, graceful and delicate you can be as you practice these exercises.

SAUTÉ

A sauté is a spring, or a jump.

- To sauté, you start with a demi-plié in 1st position, spring up into the air, and land in your demi-plié again.

Try to spring without making a sound.

- Start in demi-plié in 1st position.
- Spring into the air, straightening your legs and pointing your toes.
- Land back in your demi-plié with your knees bent.

How many sautés can you do without stopping?

Point your toes in the air.

ÉCHAPPÉ

Échappé means 'to escape'. In this movement, your feet are joined in the air, before they escape from each other as you land in 2nd position.

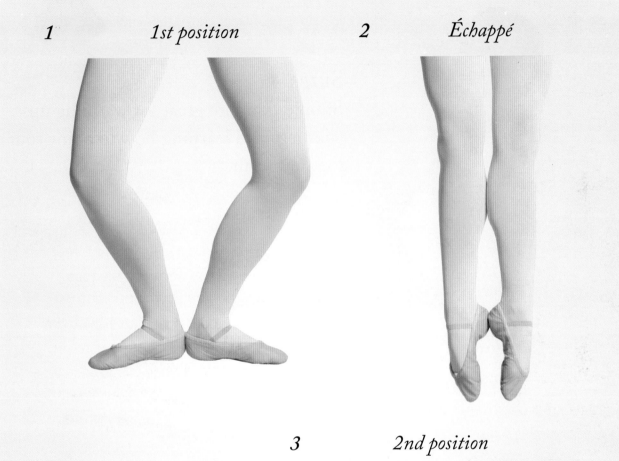

1   *1st position*

2   *Échappé*

3   *2nd position*

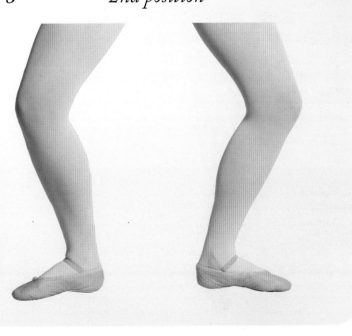

- Start with a demi-plié in 1st position.

- Spring into the air.

- Straighten your legs and allow your heels to 'escape' from each other and land in a demi-plié in 2nd position.

- Spring again and bring your heels back together to 1st position, in a demi-plié.

Skips and Gallops

Skips and gallops are a fun way to practice your jumps and learn how to move across a room.

SKIPS

Simple skips are great for warming up your legs and learning how to point your toes in the air.

- Start by skipping on the spot – raise one knee as high as you can, with the toes pointed, and hop on your supporting leg.
- Straighten your bent knee and skip on the other foot.
- Continue skipping, changing legs each time you hop.
- See how high you can jump as you skip!

Once you've mastered skipping on the spot, try skipping wherever you go.

Remember to jump as high as you can and always point your toes.

SIDEWAYS GALLOPS

Gallops are another fun way to practice your ballet!

- Start in 1st position and stretch one leg to the side.

- Hop with the other leg, step out to the side, and then jump in the air, clapping your heels together.

- Land on the second foot, with the leading foot ready to step out again.

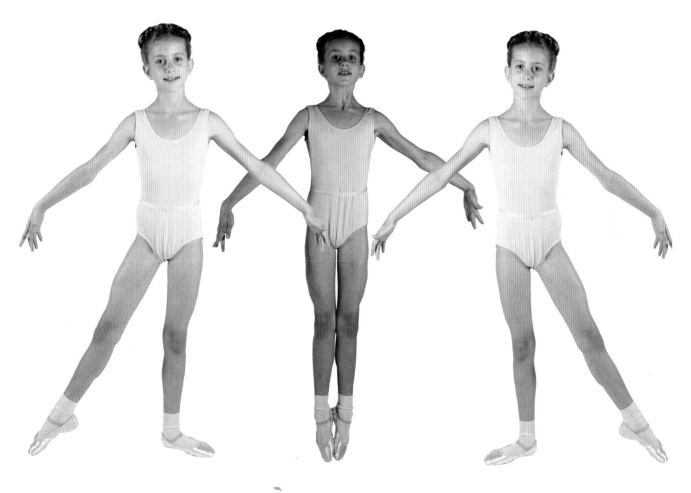

Move your legs as you gallop, and keep your back and arms still.

Point your toes in the air.

Repeat, galloping as high as you can. Once you are happy going one way, try going back the other way on the other foot.

Révérence

*A*t the end of every class, you perform a révérence, which is a curtsey (or a bow for boys), to thank your teacher, pianist, and anyone watching your class. One day you might do a révérence to thank your audience for their applause!

- Stand in 1st position, gently holding your skirt to the sides.

- Step out with one foot, pointing your toe.
- Step out with the leg nearest to your teacher.

- Take this foot back behind the supporting leg, with your toes on the floor and your heel raised.

- Bend your supporting leg, creating a window between your legs.

- Pause here for a moment.

- Straighten the supporting leg.

- Follow with a révérence to the pianist if you have one, and any other people in the room.

Make sure your back foot is fully pointed.

NOW you know your first ballet steps, put on your prettiest ballet outfit – and the lovely headband, necklace and tutu in your box, and make up your own ballet to show to your friends and family!

Arabesques

*T*he arabesque is one of the most beautiful and most famous poses in ballet. This position requires perfect balance.

To begin with, you learn an arabesque 'parterre' (this means that you have your back extended leg on the ground). Only once you have learned to perform this perfectly will you progress to lifting your leg.

Arms should form a line.

*Hold your
tummy tight.*

*Make sure your back
foot is fully pointed.*

The Ballet

It can take years of practice before you may dance on a stage. You would need to attend a special ballet school where you would practice every day.

Ballet is not just for girls, boys can also become professional ballet dancers. Male ballet dancers have to be very strong, as well as flexible, as they often have to lift the ballerinas and provide them with support when they are dancing 'en pointe'.

Pointe shoes have a special hard toe, which enables a ballerina to balance on them. It requires a lot of skill to be able to do this, and only dancers who are attending ballet classes very often are ready to be introduced to pointe shoes.

BALLERINAS use something called rosin (a white powder) on the tips of their pointe shoes to help them avoid slipping on wooden floors.

Ballet Lessons

If you enjoy ballet and would like to learn more, you can attend ballet lessons. Here, you will be taught in a class with other children, whom also want to learn more about ballet.

Ballet is very good for you for lots of different reasons. It helps to teach you to walk elegantly and to hold yourself gracefully.

Ballet lessons also involve music so you will learn about timing and learn to understand how music is used to convey feelings - such as happy and sad feelings.

Ballet helps you to stay fit and healthy, and you will make friends with other children who share your love of the dance.

Famous Ballets

A composer writes the music that the orchestra will play in a ballet. A choreographer decides which steps will be put together to form the dances in a ballet. Many ballets are based on traditional fairy tales.

CINDERELLA

This famous fairy tale was written by Charles Perrault and Sergei Prokofiev wrote the music for the ballet. Many different people have created choreography for this ballet, but Frederick Ashton is the most famous.

SLEEPING BEAUTY

This is also a fairy tale written by Charles Perrault. Peter Ilyich Tchaikovsky wrote the music for this ballet and Marius Petipa created the choreography.

THE NUTCRACKER

A Christmas story brought to life through ballet with music written by Peter Ilyich Tchaikovsky and choreography by Lev Ivanov.

GISELLE

This very famous ballet tells a romantic story, with music written by Adolphe Adam and choreography by Jules Perrot.

SWAN LAKE

Probably the most famous and well-loved ballet, with music written by Peter Ilyich Tchaikovsky and choreography by Marius Petipa.

COPPELIA

A romantic story with music by Leo Delibes and choreography by Arthur Saint-Leon.

Try to make up your own ballet using the positions in this book and act out a story.

Glossary

A

À la seconde
À la seconde means to the side.

Arabesque
The arabesque is one of the most beautiful and most famous poses in ballet. This position requires perfect balance.

B

Barre
A rail that you use while practicing certain exercises to help you balance.

Barre work
Exercises practised at the barre are one of the most important aspects of a ballerina's training and practice, focusing on most areas of the body.

Battement tendu
A movement in which one leg slides out to its fully extended position, with the toes fully stretched on the floor.

Bras bas
This is the starting position for your arms.

C

Choreographer
A choreographer decides the steps that will be put together to form the dances in a ballet.

Composer
A composer writes the music that the orchestra will play in a ballet.

D

Demi-plié
A position in which the knees are half bent and the heels remain on the floor.

Derrière
Behind

Devant
In front

E

Ecarte
A basic pose in which the dancer's leg is in second position, but the whole body is placed diagonally to the audience.

Échappé
A movement in which both legs 'escape' into an open position.

Elevation
The height achieved in any jumping movement.

F

Frog
A good warm-up exercise.

G

Grand
Large

H

Hello toes and goodbye toes
An exercise to warm up and stretch your feet!

J

Jambe
Leg

P

Pas
Step

Pas de deux
A dance for two people.

Pied
Foot

Plié
A bending of the knee or knees.

Pointe tendu
When the leg is extended and stretched so only the tip of the toes are on the floor.

Pointes, sur les
The raising of the body on to the tip of the toes.

Port de bras
Movement of the arms through various arm positions.

R

Révérence
A curtsey or bow to thank the teacher, pianist, guests and audience at the end of a performance.

Rosin
A white powder ballerinas use on the tips of their pointe shoes to help them avoid slipping on wooden floors.

S

Sauté
A spring or jump.

Soloist
A dancer who performs on their own.

Stretching
Exercises to warm up your muscles and increase your flexibility.

Supporting leg
The leg that you are standing on, which is taking the weight of your body while your other leg is moving.

Sur
On or upon.

T

Tendu
Stretched

Turn out
The way the feet and legs should be turned out from the hip joints to give the necessary freedom or movement to perform the steps of classical ballet.

Index